# THE PURPOSE OF MAN

# THE PURPOSE OF MAN

**GOD CREATED MAN AND GAVE HIM DOMINION AND AUTHORITY OVER ALL OF HIS CREATION**

**NINTH ANNIVERSARY EDITION**

JEANITA JINNAH

Nayla Book Publishers
Michigan

Nayla Book Publishers
P.O. Box 80714
Lansing, MI 48908
naylabookpublishers.com

*We exist to provide quality Christian Books to the masses. We seek to honor God by producing and publishing divinely-inspired material that express the heart of God.*

The Purpose of Man
Copyright © 2015, 2024 by Jeanita Jinnah

All Scripture quotations, unless otherwise noted, are taken from the *Holy Bible: King James Version*®. KJV®. Copyright © 1976 by Thomas Nelson, Inc. All rights reserved. Other quotations are from the following sources: New American Standard Bible (NASB). The MacArthur Study Bible. Copyright © 2006 by Thomas Nelson, Inc. The Amplified Bible (AMP). Copyright © 1987 by The Zondervan Corporation and the Lockman Foundation. All rights reserved.

All rights reserved.
No part of this book may be reproduced, scanned, or distributed in any printed or electronic form without permission. Please do not participate in or encourage piracy of copyrighted materials in violation of the author's rights. Purchase only authorized editions.

Paperback ISBN  978-0-9863889-2-7
Ebook ISBN:  978-0-9863889-3-4

## DEDICATION

For the young widow, buried deep in grief and despair. The pain of loss has ripped a hole in your heart. How do you go on? Will you ever smile again? Will you ever enjoy a beautiful rainbow again? Then one day God lifts your bowed down head, looks you in the eyes, and says, "I'm here to take away your pain." "I'm here to mend your broken heart." "Be encouraged daughter, your weeping has endured for a long night, but now the morning has come and I'm here to give you joy."

# CONTENTS

Dedication v

Introduction ix

In The Beginning 1

Adam and Eve 11

Noah 19

Abraham 27

Israel 41

David 53

Jesus 69

Afterword 77

# INTRODUCTION

AFTER GOD CREATED THE heavens and the earth, He formed a man out of the earth, out of the dust of the ground, and told the man to rule over all of His creation (the fish, the birds, the cattle, and over all the earth). God created both a man and a woman and blessed them, giving them the ability to reproduce. He told them to fill the earth, and to subdue it. The Hebrew word for subdue is kabash (kaw-bash). It means: to conquer, subjugate, bring into bondage, force, keep under, bring into subjection. God wanted man to rule over the earth, and to keep it under his authority. God gave man this authority and put all the works of His hand into the hand of man to keep it and preserve it, just as He had created it.

God was entrusting man with this great creation. The Bible says that everything God created was good. Everything He had spoken into existence, the earth, the heavens, the seas, the trees...all of it had a function and a purpose, and that purpose was good.

But during the subsequent fall of man in the garden, the authority God had given man was lost. Sin entered the picture and man became the servant of sin, no longer the servant of God. Sin began to reign in the earth. The earth was no longer subject to man, or under man's authority. Chaos ensued and things began to fall apart. The authority God had given man began to quickly slip out of his hands. Sin is a destructive force. It not only destroys man, it also destroys and erodes the earth. The earth becomes corrupt when it is filled with sin. Our souls also become corrupt when we are stained with sin. Man loses his ability to stand in the gap as God's ambassador when his soul is corroded with sin.

When a person becomes king, there is usually a coronation ceremony with the ritual placement of a crown on the person's head, and a presentation of other items of royalty such as a signet ring or a scepter. These items signify the authority the king has as ruler over his kingdom, and over his subjects. The ceremony may include taking of vows by the new monarch and some act of homage by the new ruler's subjects, such as bowing or kneeling.

During religious coronations, the new leader or king is sometimes anointed with holy oil as a sign of the bestowing of power. Once the authority has been given to the new king to rule, everything and everyone in his kingdom becomes subject to him. What the king says goes. The king's word is final authority in every decision, and people usually defer to the king's edicts and rules.

Just as all of creation bows to God, when God transferred authority over to man to rule on His behalf all of creation was to bow to man's authority, recognizing that God had conferred His power and authority over to man. God had placed man on an earthly throne making him a ruler with subjects under him. All of God's great creation was subject to man's authority.

Whenever there is someone in a position of power there is also usually someone who sees this power and begins to envy it, often desiring this power for himself. The king has to always be on guard for those who will try to rise up and test his power, or worse, those who will try to usurp the king's power. This testing of the king's power can come from either inside or outside his kingdom. Unfortunately, not everyone in the kingdom is loyal to the king.

The serpent, in the garden, must have sensed a weakness in man when he approached Eve, testing her, to see if he might tempt her to eat of the fruit of the forbidden tree that was in the midst of the garden. The serpent may have been envious of man's authority, and resentful, desiring to have such authority for himself. The Bible says that the serpent was more subtle and crafty than any beast of the field. The serpent decided to test the authority that God had given man, and tempt him to sin against God.

As with Eve and the serpent, man will always be tempted to sin against God, to disobey His will, and to lose focus thereby not fulfilling the purpose God has given him to fulfill. But we cannot become distracted or lose our focus. Each of us has a purpose and a mission. The church has been commissioned by the Lord to introduce a lost and dying world to the Lord, and to be His emissaries in the earth. Our job is to bring the kingdom of God to earth to be experienced by all.

When I think of purpose I think of people like Zacharias and Elisabeth, John the Baptist, Mary (the mother of Jesus), and the prophet Jeremiah. An angel appeared to Zacharias, the priest, in the temple and told him that he and his wife Elisabeth would have a son. Now Elisabeth was barren, and both Zacharias and Elisabeth were advanced in age. Zacharias had prayed for a son, and the angel told him that God had heard his prayers and that he would indeed bring forth a son, but this son would be different, special. This son would be the forerunner of Jesus, the Messiah. This son would be great, and would turn the sons of Israel back to the Lord their God. He would turn the hearts of the fathers back to the children, and the disobedient to the attitude of the righteous. This son would help to prepare a people for the Lord — for the coming of the Messiah. This son would be called John.

John, who was often called John the Baptist, was the son of Zacharias and Elisabeth. John was chosen by God, prior to his birth, to prepare the hearts and minds of the people to receive Jesus Christ. The Bible said that John was baptized with the Holy Ghost in his mother's womb. He was anointed by God for a specific purpose in Elisabeth's womb.

John came preaching a message of baptism for repentance from sin. He warned the Jews that God would one day judge sin, and would pour out His wrath upon the earth and all of mankind as His punishment for sin. John told the Jews that Jesus was the only way to avoid God's judgment of sin. When the Jews sent some people to ask John who he was, if he was that prophet, John said, "I am not He." "He that comes after me is before me and He is greater than me, and I am not even worthy to unleash His shoe laces." John knew that his purpose was to prepare the way for Jesus, and that when He came John was to step aside and allow Him to take over. John said, "I must decrease so that He can increase" (John 3:30).

John led a life of purpose. When he saw Jesus, John immediately recognized Him. He knew that Jesus was the Messiah. The Lord had told John, "The one you see the Spirit of the Lord descend upon, He is the one I have sent to save His people from their sins." When Jesus was baptized, the Spirit of the Lord descended on Him like a dove. John saw this and immediately recognized Him as the Son of God. John's reaction when he saw Jesus was, "Behold, the lamb of God!" John bore witness to Jesus.

Then there was Mary, who was the one the Lord chose to give birth to the Savior. When the angel of the Lord appeared to Mary he told her that she was highly favored of the Lord.

The angel told her that the Lord had chosen her to give birth to a son, who she should name Jesus, and this son would be great. He would save His people from their sins. Mary was a virgin, and she wondered how she would have a child seeing that she had never been with a man intimately. The angel told her that the Lord would overshadow her, and she would conceive a son, and she should call His name Jesus. He shall be great, and shall be called the Son of the Highest. When Mary heard this her response was, "Behold, the handmaid of the Lord; be it unto me according to your word."

Mary submitted herself to the Lord's will for her life. And the Holy Ghost overshadowed her, and she conceived a child in her womb of the Holy Ghost and named Him Jesus, and He became great, was called the Son of God, and His death on the cross and subsequent resurrection from the dead provides salvation from sin. God's will was performed through Mary, a humble servant girl.

The Prophet Jeremiah is another example of a life destined for purpose. God told Jeremiah, *Before I formed you in the womb I knew you and approved of you. Before you were born I consecrated you. I have appointed you a prophet to the nations. I have put my words in your mouth and all that I command you to speak, speak, not being fearful or afraid.* (Jeremiah 1:5-9).

Jeremiah was a prophet to Israel. He spoke God's words to Israel, as they were given to him by God. Jeremiah became God's anointed messenger. God's divine will would be performed through Jeremiah. God told Jeremiah to prophesy to Israel: to warn, to condemn, to chastise, to encourage, and to strengthen and build up.

Israel was a rebellious nation. But God loved Israel and delivered them out of bondage from Egypt, and promised to make them a great nation, and to give them a good land, if they would obey Him and keep all of His commandments. But Israel did not obey God. They served other gods, preferring these gods over God.

God used Jeremiah to speak to Israel, to encourage them to follow Him; to warn them of God's wrath if they refused to obey Him; to let them know that God would remove His hand of protection from them if they persisted in their disobedience to Him.

But Israel did not heed Jeremiah's warnings. They

persistently disobeyed God's laws, continued serving their idols, and refused to heed any of God's warnings. For this reason, God removed His hand of protection from them, and their enemies came up against them and overtook them. They enslaved Israel, and confiscated their land and property. Israel was violated by their enemies, and they were left naked and exposed. God used Jeremiah to warn them, yet they refused to heed any of his warnings.

God's plans for man have always been good. His desire is for man to live an abundant life, and that he prosper and be in health as his soul prospers. God desires for man to live together on earth in peace and harmony. And God also desires to have fellowship with man on the earth.

When we seek the will of God for our lives, we should be willing to put our will aside, and accept God's purpose and plan for us. We should ask ourselves, what is my purpose for being? Why did God create me?

Have you ever sought God's will for your life? I've discovered that sometimes what we think is our purpose in life is not actually what God has purposed for us. Our desires, hopes, and dreams are usually self-seeking and are filled with the things *we* desire for ourselves. They make us feel better about ourselves. And sometimes they make us look better in the eyes of man. Who doesn't want to appear to have it all together? And somewhere deep down inside, no matter who we are, we feel a sense of pride when others are a little envious of us and of how we appear to have it all together. We are not too shy to pat ourselves on the back, stick our chest out, and say, "I did this." But, this is not the attitude or demeanor of one who is living out God's purpose for their life.

Open yourself up to God, surrendering fully to Him. Allow God's purpose and plan for you to be the guiding force for everything you do. And remember, God's ways are not our ways. His thoughts are not our thoughts. His ways and His thoughts are higher than ours. God's purpose for us is always good. And His plan will always lead to His will being fulfilled.

# IN THE BEGINNING

WHEN GOD CREATED MAN He also gave him a purpose. Man was created by God, in His image and in His likeness, and with the breath of God, which gives him life. God breathed into man's nostrils and man became a living soul. Without God's life-giving breath inside us we would still be a lump of clay, lifeless and devoid of purpose. A blob of clay only materializes into something special in the hands of a skillful potter. Without the potter molding it and shaping it into a beautiful vessel, the clay is useless and without any significant meaning.

God gave us life and a purpose for living. He skillfully formed man out of the dust of the ground, giving him two arms and two hands, two legs and two feet, two eyes, two ears, a nose, a mouth, a brain, and a voice. God had a purpose in mind when He created man.

The Bible says that in the beginning, God created the

heaven and the earth. The earth was formless and void, and darkness was upon the face of the earth, which was filled with water. There was no light nor was there any shape to the earth. There was no way to sustain life with the earth as it was. Then God spoke, and things began to appear.

God created land, and commanded the waters to separate from the land, giving way for vegetation to grow upon the earth. He created sea creatures for the waters, giving them a watery habitation. He created the heavens (the atmosphere) and created a sun, a moon, and stars, separating the light from the darkness, and giving light to the earth. God also created flying fowl to inhabit the new heavens, and land animals to inhabit the earth. Then God looked at everything He had created and saw that it was good. Everything was as He had ordered them to be as He spoke them into existence.

God was pleased with His creation, and rested on the seventh day from His work. This day, the seventh day, has become a sacred day, for God has blessed it and sanctified it — set it apart — because in this day He rested from all His work of creating the heaven and the earth. Just as God rested from all His labors, man has also been given a Sabbath Day, a day of rest from all of his labors, for this is a holy day. This day of rest not only affords man an opportunity to rest and, therefore, to be replenished, it also gives a rest to the earth and an opportunity for the earth to be restored and replenished from the labor and the harvest that man extracts from it. This day, the Sabbath day, is holy unto the Lord.

When we are constantly overworking ourselves not giving our bodies time to rest, we can begin to feel overstressed. When we are overstressed and overworked we feel drained and fatigued, and it's much more difficult for our bodies to be restored and replenished. And without proper nourishment, which gives us the strength we need to accomplish the things we need to accomplish, and the fuel we need to power our bodies, it becomes harder for us to recover from strenuous work and to fight off disease and sickness.

This is also true with the earth. Without proper nourishment (rain, the sun, and nutrients in the soil, which is supplied by God), and a proper rest, the earth too can become overworked and have a difficult time replenishing itself. Therefore, God created the Sabbath Day and made it a day of rest for both man and the earth.

Everything God created has a purpose, a specific function. Without purpose there would be disorder and dysfunction. God is not the author of confusion. He is an orderly God. And as such, He expects us, therefore, to pattern ourselves after Him.

## THE SUN, THE MOON, THE STARS

The Bible says that God created two lights. The greater light, the sun, to rule the day. And the lesser light, the moon, to rule the night (Genesis 1:16-18). As we know, prior to the creation of the sun and the moon, the earth was a dark mass. Without these two lights, everyone would be walking around in the dark, bumping into one another. It would also be difficult for man to see to work — to till the ground, and to collect his harvest. And without the sun providing its nourishing rays to the earth, there probably wouldn't be much of a harvest.

God's sun also provides warmth for the earth. The sun's rays also have a way of filling man's heart with happiness and goodwill. There's nothing better, and more encouraging, than a bright sunny day. Everyone wants to be outdoors enjoying the warmer weather. It's hard to feel sad when you're walking around in God's sunshine.

The moon also provides light to the earth, although it does not provide as much light as the sun. When the moon appears in the sky it is a signal to man that the workday has ended. Everyone can lay down their shovels and pickaxes, and take a break. (A much-needed break.) Families are usually reunited at the end of a long day. The children's studies and chores are over. Wives can finally take a break from the chores of the day. Everyone has been fed. The animals have all been tended to. And finally, families can come together and enjoy one another's company. Quality time spent together is nourishment for a family. There are stories told around the fire. Joyful laughter and singing. All is well in the world after everyone has put in a long, hard day. Now it's time for some well-deserved rest.

The stars are often less visible than the moon and the sun, but they still have a prominent place in the sky. The stars are often visible at night. You see them twinkling in the sky on a nice starry night. They also provide guidance and are directional in nature. It was a star that led the wise men from the east to Bethlehem to where the baby Jesus was. The star led them to His exact location, and when the wise men saw Him they fell down and worshiped Him, and presented Him with gifts of gold, frankincense, and myrrh (Matthew 2:1-11). The stars also provided guidance to travelers, leading them safely to their destinations.

God has numbered the stars and given them all names (Psalm 147:4). God also made reference to the stars in His blessing of Abraham. He made a covenant with Abraham and told him He would bless him with a son, and Abraham's seed would be as numerous as the stars in heaven (Genesis 15:5).

## FOOD/NOURISHMENT

God has provided man, and animal, with healthy foods that provide nourishment for the body. There are seeds and nuts, whole grains, fresh fruits and vegetables, and plenty of lean, healthy meats. Without this nourishment man would not have the energy to do the things he needed to do to maintain his existence here on earth. Proper nutrition equals strength, health, and vitality. This is why we should always be conscious of what we are putting in our bodies.

Today, man has sadly developed a habit of eating fast

foods, processed foods, and too much refined sugar and unhealthy fats. This all affects our bodies, in a negative way. We are also starting to see an increase in illnesses and diseases today as a result, such as high blood pressure, diabetes, heart disease, and cancer. The types of food we eat can have a negative and lasting impact on our bodies. Proper nutrition is very important for our health and well-being.

If we want to live the type of life God created us to live we should make sure we are eating the foods He has provided for us. The foods God provides helps to keep us healthy and well.

In Leviticus 11, God gave Israel a list of the animals that He considered clean and, therefore, fit for consumption. This food would supply them with vital nutrients, and it would also set Israel apart from the other nations around them who were living life according to their own standards. God's standards keep us healthy and holy. They differentiate us from others around us, and keep us in right-standing with God.

## THE ATMOSPHERIC AND ECOLOGICAL SYSTEM

A cool wind on a hot summer day, the fresh air we breathe, the sun on our backs which provide warmth, the fertile soil under our feet — all of it creates a habitable environment for man. There's also the ability for the earth to replenish itself. God put life-giving seed into plants and trees, making it possible for new plants and trees to grow after they have been tapped for food, and for wood to fuel fires and to build homes. This is a system God put in place to keep the earth supplied with the things needed to sustain life. Without these things the earth would be uninhabitable.

If God had not created the atmospheric heavens there would be no place for the birds to soar, no clouds to open up and release rain on a parched earth, no place for the sun, the moon, and the stars to reside giving light to the earth, and no place for the mountains to extend as they reach up to the heavens displaying their majestic beauty.

If God had not created the oceans and the lakes, which are teeming with wildlife and flora and all manner of vegetation, there would be no way for the oceanic animals to survive and thrive, providing food for the earth, and no rivers or streams where the oceans and lakes can deposit their outflow. Fishermen would not be able to make a living. Families would starve.

God has provided a way to supply the earth with what it needs. When He created the earth He also created a system to maintain it. And because of this, the earth is still thriving today.

# ADAM AND EVE

SO WHAT IS THE purpose of man? God created man to stand guard over what He had created. Man was created to take authority over, and to maintain all of God's creation. Man is to represent God on the earth (His will, His plan, His purpose). God created the man and placed him in charge of the works of His hands. He gave man dominion over the earth, the fish of the sea, the fowl of the air, the cattle, and every thing that creepeth upon the earth, and told man to subdue it and to replenish the earth. Everything God created was good, and man was to see to it that everything remained that way, just as God had created it.

God created Adam, and Eve, his help mate, and gave them a special place to dwell on the earth — in the garden. God planted a garden eastward, in Eden, and placed Adam and Eve in the garden. There was a river that flowed out of the garden and split into four rivers (Pison, Gihon, Hiddekel, and Euphrates), and surrounded certain areas of the earth. There was also a *Tree of Life* in the garden, and a *Tree of the Knowledge of Good and Evil*. God told Adam that he could eat from every tree in the garden *except* from the *Tree of the Knowledge of Good and Evil*. God provided everything the man needed to live in the garden.

When God created the animals he brought them to Adam to name. God also took a rib out of Adam's side, and with this rib He created a woman, whom Adam called Eve because she was the mother of all living.

Adam and Eve had an innocent love for each other. They were partners together on the earth. God made them co-equals. It wasn't until they disobeyed God and ate from the tree in the midst of the garden, which God had forbidden them to eat from, that God told Eve that her desire would now be to her husband, and he would rule over her (Genesis 3:16). But before this, they were partners together in standing guard over and tending to all that God had created. God had given them authority to rule on His behalf.

The land that Adam and Eve had dominion over was teeming with wildlife. There was beauty surrounding them. I can imagine the rivers were so crystal clear that you could see right through to the bottom. There was no pollution or fog. The trees never shed their leaves, leaving them bare and exposed. Adam and Eve never experienced a tornado or an earthquake in the garden. These things just didn't exist in God's new world. There was no fear of being struck by lightning. As of yet it had never rained upon the earth (God sent a midst up from the ground to water the garden), so they never experienced the drenching rain upon their skin. The animals were not in fear of being eaten by predators. The lamb could lay down with the lion without fear of being torn to pieces by him, becoming his next meal. Everything was beautiful and peaceful on earth until the sly serpent tempted Eve.

We'll probably never know if this was the first time Eve was approached by the serpent in this manner, or if he had approached her several times before. The Bible doesn't say how many times Eve had rebuffed the serpent's suggestions that she take a bite of the fruit from the *Tree of the Knowledge of Good and Evil,* that was in the midst of the garden. But we do know that, for whatever reason, she was not able to resist him this time.

Suddenly, Eve began to see the forbidden fruit differently. She saw that it was good for food, and that it might make one wise. The serpent told her that if she ate from the tree she wouldn't *surely* die, for the only reason God doesn't want you to eat from this tree is because He knows that the moment you do, you will become as wise as He is. And don't you want to be *wise*, Eve? But, of course, the moment Eve ate of the fruit, and gave it to Adam to eat, they both died a spiritual death. From that moment, they experienced a spiritual and intimate separation from God that could only be restored by the blood of Jesus Christ. This disobedience stripped them of the authority God had given them to be His representatives in the earth.

How can we represent God when there is sin in our lives? How can we say we represent God when we disobey Him? Disobedience and sin is lawlessness (1 John 3:4). It's a refusal to obey God's laws. Adam and Eve were now outlaws, and as such, God threw them out of the garden and stationed cherubim and a flaming sword which turned in every direction at the entry to the garden to keep them out. God did not want them, in their now sin-stained condition, to stretch forth their hands and eat from the *Tree of Life,* which would have caused them to live forever in their sinful state. They had to die for their sins.

Because of Adam and Eve's sin, God pronounced a curse on the earth. The ground was now cursed, and it brought forth thorns and thistles. Man would now have to labor for his food by the sweat of his brow. Prior to this, God had given man his food freely. He had his choice of the ripe fruit from the trees in the garden, and of the herbs of the field.

God also told Eve that she would now labor in childbirth. She would bring forth her children in great pain. Her husband would also rule over her. He would be her head, her authority figure, since she had proven that she could not be trusted with authority of her own.

The serpent also did not escape God's punishment. God called him cursed above all animals (both domestic and wild), and from now on he would crawl on his belly, forever tasting the dirt of the ground, which was now cursed. God would put enmity between the woman and the serpent, and between her seed and his seed, and her seed would tread the serpent's head underfoot, and the serpent would lie in wait and bruise his heel

(Genesis 3:14-15). Today, there is now a bitter relationship between man and snakes. They are enemies.

God's laws are given for man to obey. If we obey all of God's laws, it keeps us out of sin and in God's good graces. His protection is provided for all those who obey Him and walk upright before Him. When we step away from God's laws, we are also stepping out from under His protective shield.

Adam and Eve experienced God's provision and protection in the garden. But after they sinned against Him and disobeyed Him, God threw them out of the garden and they were exposed to things they had never experienced before in the garden.

Giving into the temptation to sin not only exposes us to more sin and lawlessness, it also stirs up God's anger, removes His protective shield from around us, and similar to Adam and Eve's situation, strips us of our God-given authority to be His emissaries. We prove to God that we cannot be trusted with authority.

Our disobedience also makes us more vulnerable to Satan's lies and deception. When we disobey God we bring a curse on ourselves. Adam and Eve experienced this curse when God threw them out of the garden, forcing them to learn to survive on their own outside the protective covering of the garden. They were exposed to death, sickness, disease, and lack for the first time. They had never experienced these things before when they were living in the garden. The garden was an earthly representation of heaven for man.

# NOAH

AFTER ADAM AND EVE sinned, they began to produce seed and to populate the earth. Over time, when man began to marry and to produce offspring the earth became populous and increasingly wicked. Sin began to reign on the earth. Everything that the man thought to do, he did it. His very heart and his imaginations were wicked. Man became lustful and took wives of as many women as they chose. The earth was filled with violence. Man had successfully corrupted God's good earth.

As wickedness increased in the earth, God regretted that He had made man, and His heart became grieved. Finally, God said, "I will destroy man whom I have created from the face of the earth; both man, and beast, and the creeping thing, and the fowls of the air; for it repenteth me that I have made them" (Genesis 6:7).

But one man, Noah, found grace with God. Noah was a

righteous man who was blameless, and he walked according to all of God's ways. Noah kept God's laws, and he feared (reverenced) God. When God decided that He would destroy the earth, He made a covenant with Noah. God told Noah that He was going to protect Noah and his family from the flood, by which He had determined to destroy the earth.

God told Noah to build an ark, and gave him the measurements and the dimensions of the ark that He wanted Noah to build. God told Noah that He was going to send a flood upon the earth to destroy it along with all flesh, man as well as beast. Everything on the earth would die. But Noah and his family could find safety and God's protection from the flood in the ark.

God would also preserve some animals from the flood. God told Noah to take the animals, of every kind, a male and a female, and bring them into the ark with him and his family. God instructed Noah to take of the clean animals by sevens, the male and his female, and of every animal that was not clean, by twos, a male and his female. This was done to preserve seed after the flood.

Once Noah had completed construction of the ark, God

told him to take his wife, his three sons (Shem, Ham, and Japheth) and their wives, and the animals, and enter the ark. Once they were all safe inside the ark, it began to rain upon the earth. And the rain proceeded for forty days and forty nights. And everything on the face of the earth was destroyed. Noah was 600 years old when God sent the flood.

Once the rain had stopped, and the water had receded from the earth, Noah and all that was with him in the ark came forth out of the ark. (In total, Noah and his family were in the ark 1 year and 10 days.) Noah then built an altar unto the Lord, and took of every clean beast and of every clean fowl, and offered them up on the altar to God. When God smelled the smoke from the altar, it was sweet in His nostrils. God then said in His heart that He would never again curse the ground for man's sake, or send a flood to destroy the earth and all flesh.

God then made a covenant with Noah. He told Noah and his family to be fruitful and to repopulate the earth, both man and beast. God also told Noah that He would never again bring a flood upon the earth to destroy all flesh. And as a sign of His covenant with Noah, God would put His rainbow in the sky whenever He sent a cloud or rain on the earth. This rainbow would remind God of His promise to never destroy the earth again with a flood. Then God sent forth Noah and his family, and the animals, and blessed them, and told them to replenish the earth.

By preserving the seed of a righteous man I'm sure God had hoped that Noah's influence in the earth would be so great that his seed after him would also be righteous and, therefore, pleasing to God. God had destroyed the wickedness that was on the earth when He sent the flood to destroy the earth, along with all of mankind, who had so corrupted the earth.

## AFTER THE FLOOD

Noah and his family wasted no time establishing a new life for themselves after the flood. Noah became a farmer, and planted a vineyard. And one day, Noah became drunk when he drank of the wine from his vineyard. When Ham, his youngest son, saw his father drunk in his tent, and that he was naked, he called his two brothers, Shem and Japheth, and told them of their father's nakedness. But Shem and Japheth took a garment and laid it on their shoulders and walked backwards to place the garment on their father to cover his nakedness. They did not look at their father's nakedness, as Ham had done.

When Noah had awoken from his alcohol-induced sleep he knew what Ham, his youngest son, had done and said, "Cursed be Canaan; a servant of servants shall he be unto his brethren" (Genesis 9:25). Ham was the father of Canaan, who became the father of the Canaanites. So Noah cursed Ham's seed because of what he had done.

Through Noah and his wife, their three sons, and their wives, the earth was once again populated. At that time, everyone spoke one language, and there was only one race of people. As they began to journey through the earth, they found a valley and decided to settle there and build a city with a tower that reached up to the sky. They had determined that they would make a name for themselves in the earth.

When God saw what they were doing, and saw that there was nothing that they wouldn't do once they had set their hearts to it, He confused their language, making it difficult for them to understand one another. This put a stop to the building of their city, and their tower, and caused them to begin to disperse and to spread out one from another on the earth. Noah lived 350 years after the flood, and died at age 950.

Noah and his family were God's emissaries in the earth. God chose one man, Noah, a righteous man, to maintain the seed of man in the earth after the flood. God sent the flood to cleanse the earth of corruption, and the decay that had taken over the earth. God was angered by what He saw, and was determined to rid the earth of this corruption, and the sin and the immorality that was in man's heart.

By destroying the wickedness of man, and his seed, God saw an opportunity to plant new seed on the earth through the seed of a righteous man, Noah. But even the seed of this righteous man eventually became corrupt and wicked. Over time, the earth was once again filled with sin and degradation, as man continued to violate God's laws, living according to his own laws.

How God tolerates the willful disobedience of man, I do not know. This shows us the true nature of God. He is indeed long-suffering, and full of mercy. His love for mankind far surpasses human comprehension. God is faithfully committed to, and 100% invested in His creation. He's willing to bear through our faults in the hope that He can save us from ourselves — from our humanly wicked hearts. God hopes that

His love will be enough to change us and to cause our hearts to return to its original, sinless and eternally obedient state, as it was prior to the fall of man. Therefore, He chastises us. He warns us. He forgives us. Then He removes the stain of sin from our lives through the blood of Jesus Christ. He accepts us back into the fold. He loves us. He cherishes us. He calls us His own. Everything is good until man slips off into sin again, casting God's loving arms from around him, determining to live by his own rules and standards rather than live by God's. God's love is therefore once again rejected by man until he is once again riddled with guilt and shame, and seeks God for forgiveness, which God gives freely.

God gives us His forgiveness as often as we earnestly seek it. But unfortunately, it's not long before man falls back into sin, and separates himself, once again, from the Father. This creates a vicious cycle of sin and disobedience, then guilt and shame, followed by God's forgiveness and the restoration of man. But how long does God continue to tolerate this? How often should He keep forgiving us, especially if we are not sincere enough to *remain* faithful to Him?

We become just like disobedient Israel, who experienced

God's power and saw His love in action when He delivered them safely from Egypt, and sustained them in the wilderness 40 years. But even though Israel saw and experienced God, they still could not, would not, remain faithful to God. They shunned the God of all-power, and went whoring after other gods. Israel refused to remain faithful to God. Israel was in love with their idols, and they preferred these idols to the true and living God. They wanted to live by their own set of rules, while rejecting God's rules and commandments. Israel kept resisting God and pushing Him away.

For centuries, man has persistently and habitually failed God, rejected His love, and tried His patience. But I'm so thankful that God hasn't given up on us, yet. His love and devotion to man is real, and His mercy is long-lasting. Thank God for His mercy.

# ABRAHAM

THROUGH SHEM'S LINEAGE (the son of Noah) came another man that God would make a covenant with; Abraham, whose name at the time was, Abram. Abram and his family lived in Ur, which was an ancient city of Mesopotamia, located southeast of Babylon. Abram's father, Terah, had three sons: Abram, Nahor, and Haran. Haran, who is the father of Lot, died in Ur.

Terah decided to leave Ur for the land of Canaan. He took his surviving sons, Abram and Nahor, and their wives and families, and eventually settled in Haran, which is mid-way between Ur and Canaan. They never made it to Canaan.

Nahor married Milcah, his brother Haran's daughter (Nahor's niece). And Abram married Sarai, who was barren, and they had no children. Sarai was a beautiful woman, and was also the daughter of Abram's father but she was not the daughter of his mother, so they were also sister and brother.

The Lord appeared to Abram and told him to leave his family and his country, and to go into a land that God would show Him. God told Abram that He would bless him, and make him a great nation. Abram's name would be great and the Lord would make him a blessing, and bless all those who blessed him, and curse all that cursed him. Abram obeyed God, and left his family and his country for Canaan, the land that God had promised to give him, taking Lot, his nephew, with him.

God showed Abram all the land of Canaan, and told him that He would give Abram this land. (This is the same land that Abram's father Terah was trying to reach when they left Ur before settling in Haran.) But God told Abram that He would give this land to Abram and his descendants.

Because there was a famine in Canaan, Abram and his family eventually went down to Egypt to live there until the famine was over. While in Egypt, the Lord blessed Abram with wealth. Abram acquired silver, gold, sheep, oxen, donkeys, menservants, maidservants, she-donkeys, and camels. Abram was a very rich man.

When Abram left Egypt with his wife Sarai and all their

household, he took his nephew Lot with him. Lot was also very rich. When it was determined that the land could not hold the combined wealth of Abram and Lot, the two of them decided to separate from one another. When Lot looked and saw all the plain of Jordan and saw that it was good land, he chose to settle there, and moved his tent as far as the city of Sodom and dwelt there. The Bible says the men of Sodom were very wicked, and were sinners (Genesis 13:13).

## THE COVENANT

When Abram was 99 years old, the Lord appeared to him and confirmed His covenant with him (Genesis 17). He told Abram that he would have a son with Sarai, and that his name should be called Isaac. And although God would bless Ishmael — the son Abram bore with Hagar, Sarai's maid — and multiply his seed upon the earth, His covenant would be with Isaac; and this would be an everlasting covenant.

As a token of the covenant, God instructed Abram to circumcise every male born in his house, and every male bought with money. This would be a sign of God's covenant with Abram from generation to generation. Abram did as instructed, and every male in his household was circumcised, starting with Abram, who was 99 years old at the time of his circumcision. Ishmael (his son with Hagar, Sarai's maid) was 13 years old when he was circumcised. God also changed Abram's name to Abraham (father of a multitude). And He changed Sarai's name to Sarah (Princess).

The Lord appeared to Abraham again, along with two of His angels, and told him that by this time next year Sarah would have a son. Sarah, who overheard this commentary, laughed within herself. She thought it highly unlikely that at her advanced age she could conceive and bare a child. But the Lord said that she would indeed have a son for nothing was impossible for God.

The Lord also revealed to Abraham His intentions to destroy the cities of Sodom and Gomorrah. The degree and magnitude of sin found in these two cities had risen up to God, and had kindled His anger. Therefore, God had determined to destroy these cities, along with all of their inhabitants.

When the Lord had revealed His intentions to destroy the cities to him, Abraham asked God if He would also destroy the righteous along with the wicked? Abraham knew that his nephew Lot and his family were inhabitants of Sodom, therefore, his concern for his nephew was great. But the Lord told Abraham that if He found 10 righteous men in these cities He would not destroy the cities. The iniquities in Sodom and Gomorrah were so great that God could not find 10 righteous men in all of them (Genesis 18:16-33).

## SODOM AND GOMORRAH DESTROYED

The two angels visited Lot in Sodom, and warned him to take his wife, and his two daughters, and flee the city because the Lord was going to destroy both Sodom and Gomorrah. But He could not destroy them until Lot and his family had been removed and taken to safety. Once they were safely out of the city, the Lord rained down fire and brimstone from heaven and destroyed both Sodom and Gomorrah, along with all of their inhabitants. But when Lot's wife stopped to look back at the cities, she was turned into a pillar of salt.

Once again, God poured out His wrath upon the earth, as He had done with the flood that destroyed the whole earth in Noah's time. But this time, instead of a flood, God chose to destroy two wicked cities with fire and brimstone.

God abhors sin and disobedience. From the beginning, man has disobeyed God, stirring up God's anger and subsequent wrath. But Abraham was a righteous man, and found favor with God. God chose Abraham and his seed to be the people through which He would make a great nation of people to represent Him (His will, and His plans) on the earth. God would bless this nation of people, make them great, and provide protection and provision for them. God was hoping to establish a people for Himself who would be unlike any other nation on the earth. They would be different, separate, and a peculiar (special) people. And Abraham was just the person through whom He would establish this nation.

## THE CHOSEN SEED

Abraham was God's chosen seed. And God blessed this seed. The seed of this righteous man became a great nation. When God chooses to bless us, it is so that we can be a blessing to others. Through us, the world should know that we serve a great God. The world should become acquainted with God's power and majesty, through us. God's light should shine brightly through us.

God told Abraham that He would give to him, and his seed after him, the land of Canaan. Canaan was a good land. It was well-watered and situated in a valley on a plain. Canaan would become Abraham's new homeland. In this good land God would dwell among his people. His great power and provision would be manifested through them. The nations around them would be able to see, through Abraham's seed, how the living God interacted with man. His great love for humanity would be revealed through His demonstrated love for His chosen people. Abraham and his seed were to help spread God's light to the world so that the world, through them, would come to know the true and living God.

We are to bring God's kingdom — which is eternal in the heavens — to earth to be experienced by all. We are to show the world what God's eternal kingdom looks like. God's kingdom is holy, righteous, just, and pure. Our job, as a body of believers, is to lead the lost and dying to the only God who can save them, heal them, and deliver them from bondage. Without God, the world is hopelessly lost. But unfortunately, the world doesn't know this. The world doesn't know that Jesus *is* the only way, so it is up to us to tell them, to show them. Our lives must be lived in such a way to bring the world to the feet of Jesus.

The way Abraham lived his life brought glory to God. Abraham's life is also an example for believers today. The Bible said that Abraham believed God, and it was accounted to him for righteousness. When God spoke to Abraham and told him to leave his family, and his homeland, for a land that God would show him, Abraham trusted God, not knowing where he was going or what awaited him there in this new land.

For many, having family around gives them a sense of security. Families support one another, and help one another through difficult times and hardships. But once Abraham left his family for the new land God was taking him to, he left all of this behind.

## MY JOURNEY OF FAITH

I can remember a time when I was contemplating leaving my home in Illinois (where I was living alone at the time after the death of my husband), and moving back to Michigan to be closer to my family. At this time, I had not lived in Michigan for over 13 years. When I married my husband I left my family home in Michigan to move to Illinois with my husband. My husband and I had established a new home for ourselves in Illinois. Illinois was now our new home, and our new normal. But a few years after he passed away from cancer, I started thinking about moving back to Michigan to be closer to family once again. At the time, I was a little afraid and uncertain of making this move. What would I do in Michigan? How would I support myself?

The economy in Michigan had not been good for quite some time. When General Motors and the automotive industry started to decline, Michigan was greatly impacted, and the economy and living conditions there were so badly affected that they also began a steady decline.

I also wondered at the time if I was making the right decision because I always saw moving back to Michigan as taking a step backwards instead of moving forward. And at this time in my life, I desperately needed to move forward. So I agonized over this decision. I prayed a lot, and even shed a few tears. I think I wanted some kind of assurance from God that I was doing the right thing in moving back to Michigan.

And I wanted these assurances up front, prior to my move. I also wanted to have a job and a home secured prior to leaving Illinois.

But unfortunately, things didn't quite happen as I would have liked. It was nearly impossible for me to search for a job and a home in Michigan while I was still living in Illinois. I would need to take a lot of time off work to do an adequate job and home search in Michigan. So I saw that if I wanted to make this move I would have to just walk by faith, trusting that God would make a way for me when I got to Michigan.

At the time, I was starting to feel this strong tug drawing me back home to Michigan. I felt as if God was leading me back there. God knew that what I needed most, at the time, was the love and support of my family to aid in my healing process. And I believe that God was also teaching me to trust Him.

When we walk by faith, as Abraham did, and as I did with my move to Michigan, we usually don't have a blueprint laid out in front of us that maps out every detail of our future. And this is often what we want. We want God to tell us His plan, and to show us exactly how His plan will unfold. We want to have these things mapped out for us *before* we step out on faith. But this isn't faith. Faith sometimes leaves us in the dark daring us to trust God even when we don't know all the how's and the why's — when we don't have all the answers up front. With faith, you simply trust God — that He has all the details worked out, and a plan to bring His divine purpose for your life into fruition.

I've often heard people use the phrase "blind faith." They equate faith with walking in the dark, not having any assurances of where you're going or what you're going to do when you get there. But if you really think about it, and the Bible confirms this, faith *is* your confidence and assurance that God has everything mapped out for you.

"Faith is the *substance* of things hoped for, and the *evidence* of things not seen" (Hebrews 11:1). Faith makes things tangible. The things you couldn't normally see become visible to you when you view them through the eyes of faith. That thing you want to touch and feel, because you will only believe it's real once you have it in your hands and can touch it, becomes tangible and visible through faith. Faith is your evidence that the thing you are hoping for, and believing for, is real.

When God told Abraham that he and his barren wife would have a son, at their advanced age, Abraham believed God; and at that moment he stepped out of the natural realm, where there are limitations and barriers, and entered the faith realm, where there are no limitations or barriers. Faith made the impossible, possible. And through faith, Abraham and Sarah's dead bodies came alive, and conceived, and gave birth to a son. Faith moved the barriers out of the way.

When God speaks, we are to simply believe. Trust that God is able to do what He says He will do. Abraham believed and it was so, and it was accounted to him for righteousness. His hope and trust were securely wrapped up in God.

Let Abraham's life be an example for you. An example of what it means to believe God in the midst of impossible situations. For the Bible clearly states that *nothing* is impossible with God. If we don't believe this, it would be difficult for us to serve God. To serve God is to know Him, and to love Him, and to trust Him, and to put all of our confidence in Him. Without complete confidence in God, we are of no use to Him. Because when He speaks, instead of acting immediately on

His word, we will begin to pause, to panic, and to question everything He's said to us. God cannot use us in this state of fear. And that's exactly what doubt is: fear. Fear that God will not keep His promises. Fear that perhaps the thing we are hoping and believing God for will not come to pass. Fear that God's word will indeed return back to Him void, not accomplishing the thing that He sent it to accomplish. Fear is debilitating and harmful; it is like kryptonite to a believer. Fear renders us ineffective and powerless.

I think it's worth noting here that Abraham was 75 years old when he left his family and his home in Haran heading for Canaan, the land God had promised to give to him and his descendants. God told Abraham that he would have a son, and that he should call his name, Isaac. When Isaac was born Abraham was 100 years old. So Abraham waited 25 years for God's promise to be fulfilled. There was a little hiccup along the way, some moment of doubt on Sarah's part because she convinced Abraham to lie with her maid, Hagar. And through Hagar Abraham had a son, whom they named Ishmael. Abraham was 86 years old when Ishmael was born. But Ismael was not the promised seed. Isaac was the son God had promised Abraham and Sarah. God also blessed Ismael and made him a great nation, but it was through Isaac that God's promise to Abraham would be fulfilled.

Even if the thing God has promised us doesn't materialize overnight, we should still trust that God will bring it to pass. If He said it, He is well able to do it. It's easy to grow weary in the waiting and decide to take matters into our own hands, as Sarah did with her maid Hagar. But this only complicates things adding unnecessary heartache and grief.

God does not move according to our timetable. His timing is not necessarily our timing. God does have a purpose for each and every one of us, and in addition to this purpose He also has a set time for when His purpose will be fulfilled. Wait on God, and trust Him in the process.

# ISRAEL

ISRAEL WAS GOD'S "chosen people." God said that He would bless them, put His name in their hearts, and they would be His people, and He would be their God. The people of Israel were the descendants of Jacob, who was the son of Isaac, who was the son of Abraham. God changed Jacob's name from Jacob (supplanter, trickster) to Israel, which means, contender with God (Genesis 32:27).

Israel was a nation of Jewish people that God raised up and made into a great nation. The Bible says that they were the least, numerically speaking, of all the nations around them (Deuteronomy 7:7). So God did not choose them because they were great. But in choosing them, and blessing them, God made them great.

The people of Israel were enslaved in Egypt for 430 years. They were initially welcomed guests in Egypt, but over time, as Israel grew in number and became a great presence in

Egypt, they began to be perceived as a threat and were made slaves by Pharaoh.

Joseph, who was one of the twelve sons of Jacob (Israel), was favored by his father over all his brothers. This made his brothers hate him. When they saw that their father loved Joseph more than his brothers they began to devise plans to punish him. They were also put off by Joseph's dreams, which often portrayed his brothers as his servants. For example, Joseph told his brothers about a dream he had in which the sun, the moon, and the eleven stars bowed down to him. When Joseph told the dream to his father, Jacob rebuked him and said to him, "What is this dream that thou hast dreamed? Shall I and thy mother and thy brethren indeed come to bow down ourselves to thee to the earth?" (Genesis 37:9-10). This unsettled his brothers, and they envied him and began to call him "the dreamer," and devised a plan to get rid of him. But Jacob took special note of his son's dream.

Eventually, Joseph was sold into slavery by his brothers. They sold him to Ishmaelite traders — for twenty pieces of silver — who were on their way to Egypt to do business there. Their hatred and jealously of Joseph had blinded them, and caused them to turn against their own brother. But God favored Joseph and blessed him during his captivity in Egypt; and after a period of time, during his servitude, Pharaoh saw that the hand of the Lord was on Joseph, and that the Lord had given him the spirit of wisdom, and the ability to interpret dreams, so he placed Joseph as governor over the land of Egypt. All of Egypt came to bow down to Joseph, this Hebrew slave. And Pharaoh prospered under Joseph's governorship.

Over time, Joseph and his father Jacob were reunited. Jacob had always assumed that Joseph was dead, because this is what his brothers told their father after they sold Joseph to the Ishmaelite traders.

There was a famine in the land of Canaan, and Egypt was the only place where there were still food supplies. During this time, Egypt was under the governorship of Joseph, who had wisely stored up provisions in Egypt in preparation for the famine, which God had revealed to Pharaoh in a dream, which Joseph later interpreted for him (Genesis 41).

When Jacob sent his sons to Egypt to buy food, they found their long lost brother Joseph there alive and in good health, and in a position of power over all the land of Egypt. When

Joseph learned that his beloved father Jacob was still alive he sent for him to come down to Egypt, along with all of his household, and live with him in the land of Egypt, where there was an abundant supply of food.

So in the end, Joseph was used by God to preserve the lives of His father, his brothers, and their households; and they had a new-found respect for Joseph, and they bowed down to him, as was revealed to him in the dream he had years prior. God was showing Joseph in this dream how He would raise Joseph up to greatness, and use him to protect and to preserve the heritage of the Jews so the promise He made to Abraham would be fulfilled. While they were in the land of Egypt, God not only preserved them, He also prospered them.

Through the course of time, the old Pharaoh died, and there was another Pharaoh who began to reign in Egypt who did not know Joseph or his family. When this new Pharaoh saw that the children of Israel were mighty in number and that they had acquired much wealth, he viewed them not as the previous Pharaoh had viewed them, but began to perceive them as a threat to his kingdom, and to Egypt, so he enslaved them giving them difficult and burdensome tasks to complete.

Israel's burden in Egypt became so great that they began to cry out to God to deliver them. And God did deliver them. He sent Moses to be an intermediary between Pharaoh and God. God worked mighty works through the hand of Moses, and Aaron, his brother, whom God sent along to assist Moses. When God delivered Israel out of Egypt, He did so with a mighty hand. He performed many signs and great wonders in the presence of Pharaoh and all of Egypt. There was no doubt that Israel's God was a great and powerful God.

God rescued Israel from their years of servitude, and told them that He would give them a land of their own, and this land would be flowing with milk and honey. In other words, this land would be bountiful and overflowing with wealth. This land, and their relationship with God, would further separate Israel from the other nations around them who were still worshiping other gods, and living according to their own standards.

God promised to bless Israel, to protect them, and to prosper them, if they would serve Him, remain faithful to Him, and obey all of His commandments. Israel would be God's light to the earth. A holy nation. They would show the other nations what it was like to serve the one true God. God's substantial powers would be revealed through Israel, His chosen people. And God would make Israel's name great in the earth.

But sadly, just like Adam and Eve in the garden, Israel failed God. They had not come out of Egypt long before they started murmuring and complaining against God. They were not satisfied with His provisions, and let it be known that they were better provided for when they were in Egypt. God supplied them with manna (like a sweet wafer) to sustain them, but they wanted more; they wanted meat, so God sent quails into their camp to appease them, and to quiet their grumbling.

Israel continued to serve other gods in the wilderness — the same gods they had served while they were in Egypt. They simply refused to give these gods up. The Bible says that Israel was unfaithful to God, and went whoring after other gods. Because of Israel's disobedience and unfaithfulness, God made them wander in the wilderness for 40 years. God could not, would not, allow such corruption in the good land that He had promised to give them — the land of Canaan.

Israel's behavior angered God. They murmured against

Him, and complained. They were not satisfied with only serving this God who had answered their prayers and delivered them from 430 years of captivity. In the wilderness, their practice of idolatry grew increasingly worse.

Israel was also unhappy with Moses and Aaron. They wondered if they had led them into the wilderness so that they might die of starvation and thirst. No one was exempt from Israel's anger and contempt. For this reason, God called them stiff-necked and disobedient, and a rebellious nation. God would also remove His hand of protection from over them, and cause their enemies to rise up against them and defeat them.

God used other nations to bring judgment on Israel. These nations (Assyria, Babylon, Persia) removed them from their homeland, enslaved them, ransacked the temple in Jerusalem taking away the sacred treasures found in the temple. Israel had stirred up God's anger with their refusal to obey His laws.

Israel wanted a king so that they might be like the other nations around them, who also had kings. Initially, God was their ruler, their king. But they wanted a natural king like the other nations. When God told them what their lives would be like under a king — he will take your sons and make them horsemen over his chariots and commanders over his army; he will take your daughters and put them to work as perfumers, and cooks, and bakers; he will take your land, and give them to his officers and to his servants; he will take a tenth of your flocks, and you yourselves will become his servants — Israel refused to listen to God's warnings and insisted on having a king to judge over them. So God gave them a king but told them that He would not listen to their complaints when they came to Him later crying about their king.

One thing that always perplexes me about Israel is that they saw God's power when He delivered them in a mighty way out of Egypt. They saw how He dealt with the Egyptians, bringing plagues upon them, destroying them in a watery grave as they pursued Israel through the Red Sea, which God had parted causing Israel to cross over on dry ground. Israel heard God's audible voice in the wilderness. They saw His glory when He descended on the mountain, and the mountain began to smoke and quake. They experienced His provisions in the wilderness when He supplied them with manna, and when their clothes did not grow old, nor did their shoes wear out, when He led them through the wilderness for 40 years. Israel had a remarkable encounter with the living God… and yet, they still refused to serve Him. They still refused to obey His commandments. They simply refused to let go of their idols and serve the one true God. They rejected God. Israel failed God in the wilderness.

Moses told Israel that God tested them in the wilderness. He let them go hungry, and caused them to wander in the wilderness to humble them and to test them; to see if He could trust them; to see if they would obey Him. God wanted to know if He could trust Israel with His blessings. He had promised to bless Israel, make them a great nation, and give them a great land. But first, God wanted to know if they would be faithful with the blessing. God wanted Israel to remain faithful to Him. But of course, Israel failed the test — miserably. They proved to God, through their actions, that they could not be trusted with His blessings. Israel failed God.

For this reason, God rejected Israel. God decided to extend His hand to the Gentiles, who had previously been excluded by God, and who were considered unclean by the Jews, according to Jewish standards. Israel was God's chosen people, a chosen race (Jews). They were the descendants of Abraham, Isaac, and Jacob. But when they rejected God, this both hurt and infuriated Him. They also rejected Jesus as the Messiah, whom it had been prophesied would come. God then said that His offer of salvation through Jesus Christ was now open to the Gentiles. And He chose Paul to be an Apostle to the Gentiles, leading them to belief in Jesus, by which salvation comes.

Because of this, we, who were once excluded, have been extended the offer of salvation through Jesus Christ. We have been grafted in. The Bible says that some of the branches have been removed (the Jews) so that those who were once wild olive shoots (the Gentiles) could now be grafted into the vine, and given the same benefits that was once exclusively enjoyed by the original branches. Because the Jews rejected Him, everyone, not just Jews, now have a right to salvation through Jesus Christ (Romans 11).

This should not cause us to gloat. It should actually humble us. Because, if the original branches were not spared, because of disobedience and unbelief, how much more would those of us who have been grafted in be spared, should we disobey

God?

Because of Israel's disobedience and their refusal to serve God, and God's subsequent rejection of them, you and I now have a right to be called sons and daughters of the most High God. Yes, this is something that we can rejoice about, but we should also earnestly pray for the original branches — the Jews — that their stony hearts would be opened to receive God in His fullness, and that they would not continue to reject Jesus Christ as the Messiah. And we should also pray that *our* hearts do not turn to stone, and that we would not reject Jesus, as Israel has rejected Him. May we always have a mind to serve God, who is our only hope in a world filled with hopelessness.

What was Israel's purpose? To be the nation by which the Messiah would come. To be God's chosen nation of people that He would use to be a light to the other nations around them. To be a people wholly dedicated to God, obedient to Him, and blessed by Him. To be a special people that God could call by His holy name. God would put His name in their hearts, and they would be His holy people. God would show us through Israel how to serve a holy God.

Israel was also the open door by which the rest of us could come to the Lord. They paved the way for all of us to be saved. No, they did not always listen to God, and they repeatedly tested His patience. But they were the first to be chosen by God as His special people, a holy nation who would represent God's grace and mercy to the nations around them. Now we (all believers — Jews and Gentiles) have been hand-picked and chosen by God to be His special people, a holy nation that brings His light to the world. Through us the world should come to know God. We should represent Him, His love, His mercy, His grace, and His power, to the unbelieving world around us.

When we are walking in the fullness of God's grace, and obeying all of His commandments, and speaking what He tells us to speak (through His word and His Holy Spirit), the world can experience God and His powerful kingdom through us as we are His appointed and anointed ambassadors on the earth. The light of God should shine so brightly through us that the world can't help but see His glory. Through us the world can come to know, and experience God.

# **DAVID**

DAVID WAS HAND-PICKED by God to be king over Israel, after He had rejected Saul from being king. The Bible calls David, "A man after God's own heart" (Acts 13:22). God told the prophet Samuel to go to Jesse's house, in Bethlehem, and anoint one of his eight sons as the new king of Israel. God told Samuel to take a bottle of oil, and God would let him know when he got there which of Jesse's sons was to be the next king. Samuel obeyed, and when he got to Jesse's house Jesse made seven of his eight sons pass before Samuel, one-by-one, starting from the oldest.

Samuel saw that some of Jesse's sons were great in stature, and some were very good-looking. When he saw them, Samuel said within himself: surely one of these is God's chosen. But God told Samuel that He had *not* chosen any of these. While man looks at the outward appearance, God looks at and examines the heart.

After God had rejected the seven sons Jesse paraded before him, Samuel asked Jesse if he had any more sons. Jesse said, "Yes, I have one more son who keeps my sheep." When they had sent for David, who was the youngest, and Samuel looked upon him, he saw that David was ruddy (a reddish complexion), and had a beautiful countenance. Then God said to Samuel, "This is him whom I have chosen, rise up and anoint him." When Samuel had anointed David with oil the Spirit of God came upon David.

David was a skillful musician. He wrote and sang beautiful songs. He was called, "The Sweet Psalmist of Israel" (2 Samuel 23:1). After God rejected Saul from being king, the Spirit of the Lord departed from Saul and God sent an evil spirit to trouble him. When his servants saw that an evil spirit from the Lord was on Saul, they advised him to send for a man who was skillful in playing the harp who, when the evil spirit was upon Saul, could play the harp and the evil spirit would leave him. Saul agreed, so they sent to Jesse to have David come and stand before the king as his personal musician. When Saul saw David he loved him. And David loved and respected Saul.

David was fearless. While keeping his father's sheep, there was a time when a lion and a bear took a lamb from the flock. David took the lamb out of the mouth of the lion and out of the mouth of the bear, and when they went after David, he took them by the beard (fur) and killed them. David recognized that it was God who delivered him out of the paw of the lion and the bear.

## GOLIATH

There also came a time when the armies of Israel were engaged in battle with the Philistines. David's brothers were soldiers in the Israeli army. Jesse (David's father) sent David to the battle lines to take some food to his brothers, and to inquire as to their welfare. When David reached the army and had saluted his brothers, he saw a man of the Philistine army, whose name was Goliath, come out to taunt and to challenge the men of Israel. This man, Goliath, was a giant. He stood over nine feet tall. The men of Israel were deathly afraid of him, and they fled from him.

The men of Israel told David that King Saul had promised to give the man who killed Goliath great riches, the king's daughter as his wife, and to make his father's house free from taxes and service. David was indignant when he heard Goliath challenge Israel. He said, "Who is this uncircumcised Philistine that he should challenge the army of the Lord?" So David said that he would kill this man, Goliath, and rid Israel of the man who had become their tormentor.

When they took David before King Saul and told the king that this young man was willing to fight against Goliath to rid Israel of its adversary, Saul said to David, "You are not able to go against this Philistine to fight with him; you are only a child." But David told Saul of the time when he was tending his father's sheep and a lion and a bear came and took a lamb from the flock, and David snatched the lamb out of its mouth, and killed both the lion and the bear. This uncircumcised Philistine, said David, will be as one of them seeing that he has challenged the armies of the living God.

David told the king that just as God delivered him from the lion and the bear He would also deliver him out of the hand of this Philistine. Saul then said to David, "Go, and the Lord be with you." Saul had his personal armor and a helmet of brass brought to David. He also gave him a coat of mail (an armored coat made of interlinked metal rings), and gave him a sword. But David, feeling cumbersome with these weapons of war, took them off saying that he could not fight the Philistine with these things. So David took his shepherd's staff, five smooth stones, and a slingshot and went to fight Goliath.

When Goliath saw this young kid he thought it might be a joke. He belittled David and cursed him by his gods. David said to Goliath, "You come to me with a sword, a spear, and a shield but I come to you in the name of the Lord of hosts, the God of the armies of Israel, whom you have challenged" (1 Samuel 17:45).

And David took a stone from his bag, and put it in his slingshot and slung it, and the stone hit Goliath sinking deep into his forehead, and he fell to the ground upon his face. David ran and stood upon Goliath, and took Goliath's sword, and cut off his head. When the Philistine army saw that their champion was dead, they fled.

David was a hero. This little ruddy-faced boy, who had kept his father's sheep, had rid Israel of their enemy and won favor in the sight of all Israel. And King Saul honored his pledge and gave David his daughter (Michal) to wed, and

David's family also benefited from his newfound status.

Both Johnathan, Saul's son, and Michal, Saul's daughter, loved David. Johnathan and David's love for each other surpassed that of the love between a man and a woman. Johnathan loved David as he loved his own life.

Saul was jealous of David; he thought that David might next try and take the kingdom from Saul. He had already won the hearts of the people, and the hearts of his son and daughter.

Saul tried to kill David, on several occasions. But David never once stretched forth his hand against Saul to do him harm, even though he had many opportunities to do so. David recognized that even though God had rejected Saul from being king, he was still the Lord's anointed, and he would not stretch forth his hand against the Lord's anointed.

When Saul and Johnathan were killed in battle, and when the news reached David, he mourned for them. He cried and fasted until the evening. He still had respect for Saul even though Saul had tried many times to kill him. David lamented over Johnathan and Saul, and penned this song for them: "How are the mighty fallen!" David told Israel to learn the song, and to teach it to their children.

David acted wisely in all his ways, and succeeded, and the Lord was with him. David looked to God for everything and consulted God before making any decision. "Lord, should I go up..." "Should I do this..." "If I go up to battle, will you deliver my enemies into my hand?"

David insisted that everyone be treated fairly, even in battle. When the Amalekites burned their city, carried away the women and children, and looted the city, those men who stayed behind with the stuff because they were too weak to go on, were each given an equal share of the spoil that was recovered from the Amalekites. This was made a statute and an ordinance for Israel: Equal share for all (1 Samuel 30:1-25).

David desired to build a house for the Lord. He said it's not right that he should dwell in a house made of cedar while the Lord dwelled in a cloth tent. But the Lord told David that David's son, who would be a man of peace, would build Him a house.

David was a man of war. He fought many battles. He was a very courageous man. But God would give David's son rest from his enemies, and this son would build a house for the

Lord to dwell in.

God favored David, and blessed him. God told David that he had chosen him from following the sheep to be ruler of His people, Israel. He destroyed David's enemies and made his name great. God would establish David's throne forever. David's son would build the Lord a house, and God would establish his son's kingdom forever. David asked the Lord, "Who am I?" and "What is my house?" David was humbled in the presence of the Lord.

## BATHSHEBA

But in one thing did David offend the Lord — in the matter of Uriah the Hittite, and his wife Bathsheba. One day when David went up to the roof of his house, there in the distance he saw a woman, Bathsheba, bathing herself. Bathsheba was very beautiful, and David inquired as to who she was. David sent messengers and took Bathsheba and brought her into his house, and David lie with her.

Shortly after, Bathsheba sent a message to David informing him that she was with child. David, panicking at the news, sent Joab (his nephew, who was a commander of David's army) to go and fetch Uriah, Bathsheba's husband, from the battlefield and bring him to the king.

When Uriah stood before the king, David asked him for a report of the battle. When Uriah had finished speaking, David sent him away to his home hoping Uriah would go home and lie with his wife, Bathsheba. David had determined to cover up his sin of sleeping with Bathsheba by passing the child she was carrying — his child — off as Uriah's. But Uriah, an honorable man, refused to go down to his house. He thought it not right for him to go home and refresh himself and lie with his wife when his fellow-soldiers were still on the battlefield and, therefore, could not enjoy such conveniences themselves.

When David heard that Uriah had not gone home but had slept at the door of the king's house with all of David's servants, David sent for him and asked him why he had not gone down to his house. Uriah told David that it was not right that he should go to his house and eat and drink and sleep with his wife while the men of Israel slept in open fields. He said, "By your life O king, and by the life of your soul, I will not do this thing." David then tried another tactic. He gave Uriah food and drink (spirits) and made him drunk, hoping that an inebriated Uriah would make his way to his own house. But when the evening fell Uriah still did not go home; he spent another night at the king's door with the king's servants.

David, seeing that he would not be able to cover up his sin, wrote a letter to Joab (his nephew), and sent it by the hand of Uriah, to place Uriah on the front line of the fiercest battle and to withdraw from him so that he may be struck down and die. So Joab obeyed the king and placed Uriah where he knew there was heaving fighting and there were valiant men. There was a battle and some of David's men died, and Uriah the Hittite also died. So Joab sent word by a messenger informing the king that Uriah was dead.

When Bathsheba heard that her husband was dead, she mourned for him. When her mourning was over, David sent and brought her to his house and she became his wife. But this thing that David had done did not please the Lord. The Lord sent Nathan the prophet to David to rebuke him for this thing.

*7 Nathan then said to David, "You are the man! Thus says the LORD God of Israel, 'It is I who anointed you king over Israel and it is I who delivered you from the hand of Saul. 8 I also gave you your master's house and your master's wives into your care, and I gave you the house of Israel and Judah; and if that had been too little, I would have added to you many more things like these! ⁹ Why have you despised the word of the LORD by doing evil in His sight? You have struck down Uriah the Hittite with the sword, have taken his wife to be your wife, and have killed him with the sword of the sons of Ammon. ¹⁰ Now therefore, the sword shall never depart from your house, because you have despised Me and have taken the wife of Uriah the Hittite to be your wife.' ¹¹ Thus says the LORD, 'Behold, I will raise up evil against you from your own household; I will even take your wives before your eyes and give them to your companion, and he will lie with your wives in broad daylight. ¹² Indeed you did it secretly, but I will do this thing before all Israel, and under the sun.'" ¹³ Then David said to Nathan, "I have sinned against the LORD." And Nathan said to David, "The LORD also has taken away your sin; you shall not die. ¹⁴ However, because by this deed you have given occasion to the enemies of the LORD to blaspheme, the child also that is born to you shall surely die" (2 Samuel 12).*

David and Bathsheba's child indeed became very sick, and

David fasted and prayed to the Lord for the child. He refused to eat and he lay all night upon the ground. He hoped that God might change his mind and spare the child's life. But God did not spare the child, and on the seventh day the child died.

When David saw that the child was dead, he rose up, washed himself, and took nourishment, which he had previously refused. David accepted the will of God in regards to his child. He understood that he had dishonored God by his sin in taking Bathsheba, another man's wife, and having her husband killed to cover up his sin.

David and his wife, Bathsheba, comforted each other after the death of their child and they did eventually have another child, who they named Solomon. The Bible says that God loved Solomon. Solomon is the son whom God had said would build Him a house.

Solomon was a man of understanding and would become a great king; and the Lord blessed him tremendously with wisdom and great riches. Through Solomon, David's legacy continued. God had promised to bless David, his kingdom, and to make his name great. David's kingdom would be far-reaching and God would establish his throne forever.

Through David's lineage would come the Messiah, who would come and save the world from sin. The Bible calls Jesus the seed of David. Jesus said, "I Jesus have sent mine angel to testify unto you these things in the churches. I am the root and the offspring of David, and the bright and morning star" (Revelation 22:16). God told David that his seed would forever sit upon the throne. God chose David to rule over His people, Israel. And He established David's kingdom forever.

## SELECTED FOR A PURPOSE

I sometimes find myself thinking about some of the characteristics of the people God chose to use to do great things for Him. None of these people were perfect, but they all had something in them that God saw, and out of all the people He could have chosen, He chose these people.

For example, God chose Moses to deliver Israel out of Egypt. He was chosen and given the authority to approach Pharaoh on God's behalf. God put His words in Moses' mouth, and showed His mighty power through the hand of Moses. The Bible said Moses was a humble man. In fact, he was more humble than anyone on the earth. He was obedient to God, and he never tried to assert himself over God. He was God's servant and he submitted to God's will, and because of this, Israel was brought out of Egypt with great power. God was glorified, and the other nations around them feared Israel's God.

There was also Mary, whom God chose to be the vehicle through which the Saviour of the world would come into the world. I'm sure there were many virgins at the time that God could have chosen. But God saw something in Mary, and He overshadowed her with His Spirit and she conceived in her womb Jesus, who was God's anointed and appointed — His only begotten Son.

When the angel told Mary that God had chosen her to birth the Messiah, she wondered how could this happen since she was a virgin and had never known a man intimately. But Mary understood the magnitude of her calling, and she submitted to God's will, and she said, "Be it unto me according to your word" (Luke 1:38).

And of course there was David, whom God chose to establish His covenant with and to give him an earthly kingdom which would bring forth Jesus Christ, who is the

King of Kings. Jesus's kingdom has been established in heaven, and His kingdom is far superior than any earthly kingdom; and He will rule forever. David was humbled and amazed that God would even consider him. David recognized the purpose God had placed in him, and was determined to fulfill his purpose. David was not a perfect man, but he truly loved God and he put his complete trust and confidence in Him. David was indeed a man after God's own heart.

David's kingdom was an earthly reflection of God's heavenly kingdom. David's kingdom encompassed all of Israel, God's chosen people. As long as those under the king's authority and charge remained loyal to the king, they were granted the king's favor and protection. But the moment they disobeyed the king, they risked incurring the king's wrath, and also possibly being kicked out of and banned from the kingdom. If you wanted to remain in the kingdom, you had to remain obedient to the king. And if we want to remain in God's eternal kingdom, we must remain obedient to God.

Obedience and humility go a long way with God. If we want the favor of God to rest on our lives, we must humble ourselves before Him and remain obedient and submissive to His will. God has created each of us for a purpose. God's purpose is always divine, and is designed to bring about His good will.

# JESUS

THE BIBLE SAYS, "For God sent not his Son into the world to condemn the world, but that the world through him might be saved" (John 3:17). Jesus was sent to seek and to save the lost. Jesus came preaching and teaching the kingdom of God. He introduced the world to God's kingdom. This kingdom was not of the earth, but it was a spiritual kingdom. God's kingdom reflected His glory and majesty. Jesus also said He came to do the will of the Father. The Father's will was visually reflected in Jesus's actions; in everything that He did.

When Jesus healed the lepers, restored sight to the blind, raised the dead back to life, preached the gospel to the poor, and gave hope to the afflicted, He was performing the Father's will. He also taught His disciples to pray, "Thy will be done on earth, as it is in heaven." As God's earthly representative, Jesus was bringing God's will to earth through His actions.

God's will for the earth was for it to be a visual — although earthly — reflection of heaven.

There is no sickness in heaven, therefore, Jesus came to earth healing all who had the faith to be healed. There is no affliction in heaven, therefore, Jesus came setting those free who had been bound by affliction, sometimes for years. There are no diseases in heaven, so those who are bound by diseases such as diabetes, cancer, heart and lung disease, and high-blood pressure can receive healing through Jesus Christ because He's shown us, through His actions, that it is the Father's will to heal and deliver us from these diseases. Also, when God brought Israel out of Egypt, the Bible said that not one of them were feeble (Psalm 105:37). This visually reflected God's will on earth as it is in heaven, that none of His children are sick, and that all are healthy and whole.

There is also no sin in God's kingdom, so Jesus was sinless. He never gave in to the temptation to sin, although temptation was all around. Jesus resisted the temptation and was promoted by God, and is now seated at the right hand of the Father. Jesus was given a name which is above all other names. It is by this name — Jesus — that all men can be saved.

After Jesus was raised from the dead, and before He made His ascent back up into heaven, He told His disciples, "All power is given unto me in heaven and in earth" (Matthew 28:19); and He gave this same power over to His disciples to finish His work so that God's will would continue to be performed on earth.

Jesus transferred this same power over to the church. The church is now God's representatives on earth, with Jesus Christ as its God-appointed spiritual head. God placed Jesus as head over His church. Jesus's shed blood at Calvary has given us life — eternal life. He gave His life so that we might live. And God desires that we should live an abundant life. He desires that our lives visually reflect His glory, His character, and His nature. Therefore, He gives us of His Spirit, filling us up with His essence and His nature.

Those who have been Spirit-filled should take on the same characteristics of God. We should think like Him, act like Him, and our thoughts should reflect God's thoughts. Our will should be shaped by God's will. Our desire should be to do the will of the Father, who has created us and given us a purpose

— His purpose. Our purpose is to be representatives of the kingdom.

Jesus always gave glory to God, seeking no glory for Himself. He gave all praise and honor to God. He recognized that God had given Him the power and the authority to do the things He did. His faith and complete trust in God granted Him certain privileges as the Son of God. Likewise, our faith and complete trust in God grants us certain privileges as sons and daughters of God. It would behoove us to become acquainted with the rights and privileges that are available to us as God's children, and to exercise these rights and privileges.

These rights have been automatically conferred upon us, but until we become aware of them, and utilize them, they are like buried treasure yet to be unearthed. The people of God need to begin to unearth their potential, which has been buried for so long in "church doctrine," in legalism, and in some instances, carnality. If we're not walking in the fullness of God's power and living the abundant life, which He desires us to have, it's not God's fault, it's our fault.

Just as those who are born into royal families on earth, we — the church body — should come to fully embrace the status that we have been born into. "But you are a chosen people, a royal priesthood, a holy nation, God's special possession, that you may declare the praises of him who called you out of darkness into his wonderful light" (1 Peter 2:9). God sees us as royalty. Therefore, it's time for the church to start behaving like royalty. We are a part of God's kingdom. And God's kingdom is not of this earth. God welcomes all who are truly repentant into His eternal kingdom.

Our royal status in the body of Christ is not given to us to make us proud, with our chests puffed out. Jesus did not walk the earth proud, looking down His nose at others. He humbled Himself and took on the form of a lowly servant so that He might win the masses back to the Father. He did not come with pomp and circumstance (pageantry). He did not consider Himself better than anyone. He understood that His mission, His purpose in coming to earth could only be fulfilled when He sought to do the Father's will.

When we are focused on doing God's will, it's hard to focus on ourselves. When we seek to please God, we have no interest in pleasing man — becoming people pleasers. When we are living out God's purpose for our lives, God's will is being accomplished in us.

From the beginning, man has failed God. And to this day man has continued to fail God. When Jesus came to earth, born of a woman, and in the form of sinful flesh, He came as a light to man, as an example for us to follow, saying: *Let me show you how it's done. Let me show you how to represent the Father on earth.*

Jesus fully embraced God's kingdom; He showed us how this kingdom operates. Jesus showed us how to inherit the kingdom. He also showed us how one could be disinherited from the kingdom: through willful disobedience, promoting oneself above God, refusing to let go of sin, and serving other gods. No one, or no thing is to be placed above God, nor should we serve any other god but God the Father.

Jesus shed light on this kingdom, showing us that God's kingdom is far superior than man's earthly kingdom. God's will reigns supreme in His kingdom. God's throne is in heaven, and the earth is His footstool. Those who wish to become a part of God's kingdom must come through Jesus Christ. Anyone who comes any other way is a thief and a robber. Jesus is the only way to the Father.

God's love for us is so clearly evident. His desire is to restore to man all that was lost in the fall when Adam and Eve sinned in the garden. We were never created to die; we were created to live forever. We were never created to inherit sickness and disease. We were created to inherit eternal life. We were never created to experience poverty or lack. We were created to experience God's provisions, which never run out. Jesus said, "The Spirit of the Lord is upon me, because he hath anointed me to preach the gospel to the poor; he hath sent me to heal the brokenhearted, to preach deliverance to the captives, and recovering of sight to the blind, to set at liberty them that are bruised, to preach the acceptable year of the Lord" (Luke 4:18-19).

Jesus came preaching and teaching restoration. If you are broken, you can be made whole. If you are lost, you can be found. If you are hungry or thirsty, come and drink from a fountain that never runs dry. If you are bruised, you can be healed. God wants to mend your broken heart, and put it back together again. God has the cure for whatever ails you. Jesus said, "He that believeth on me, as the scripture hath said, out of his belly shall flow rivers of living water" (John 7:38). God wants to fill us with His Spirit. "Believe me that I am in the Father, and the Father in me: or else believe me for the very works' sake" (John 14:11). Simply believe.

Our message, our mission, is similar to that of Jesus's. We were created for a divine purpose. Our lives should be lived in such a way that we bring glory to God, and shine a light on God's eternal nature. Jesus said, "He that hath seen me has seen the Father" (John 14:9).

This should also be true for us, the church body. When the world looks at us they should see a reflection of the Father. If His Spirit lives in us it should be reflected in the way we live our lives. It should be reflected in the way we carry ourselves, in our actions, and in our speech. His Spirit in us brings about a change in us. We no longer live for ourselves. We live for God. To please Him. To serve Him. And to see that His will is done on earth as it is in heaven. Let's stop living for ourselves, and start living for God.

## AFTERWORD

NOW THAT WE KNOW what is expected of us as believers and followers of Jesus Christ, our very lives should be surrendered to God's will. His will should be our focus, and the thing that drives us. The thing that gets us out of bed each day. Doing the Father's will and pleasing the Father should be the thing that pumps life into our veins. After all, it is the breath of God flowing through our bodies that gives us life. He gave us life so that we might fulfill His purpose.

The Bible gives us many examples of people who were chosen by God for a specific purpose, some of which we have looked at in this book. These people had an express purpose for being, as do we. And some of these people remained faithful to God and fulfilled their purpose, and some did not. Some humbled themselves and submitted to the Lord's will, and others did not. Yet in all of this, God still remained faithful. He always kept His promise to those whom He had covenanted with. God's will will always be fulfilled, even if He has to raise up a few stones or speak through a donkey. God will always find a way for His will to be performed on earth, as it is in heaven.

From the beginning, God has always used man as His earthly representatives. He started with Adam and Eve in the garden. He formed Adam out of the dust of the ground, and took a rib out of his side and created a woman to stand alongside the man, and the two of them together were to stand guard of God's creation, until they failed Him and sinned against Him in the garden.

God then searched the earth for a righteous man to leave seed on the earth, after He had determined to destroy the earth because it had become corrupt. God found one man, Noah, who's seed He determined would repopulate the earth after the flood. But over time, the earth once again became filled with corruption. This shows us that the very nature of man is wicked. The flesh is an unruly creature, and hard to tame. This is why we must crucify the flesh, daily, and learn to walk after the leading of the Holy Spirit, and not according to the leading of the flesh. Our flesh, if left unchecked, will always lead us outside of the will of God.

Then God desired to create a nation of people who would be His special people. God determined that this nation would be a light to the nations around them. They would be different from the other nations in that this would be a holy nation. In other words, this nation would take on God's nature, which is holy. God would train them in His ways, and teach them to obey His commandments, which were designed to keep them holy. God chose one man, Abraham, and decided that this nation would come from his seed. He made a covenant with Abraham and told him that his seed after him would always be under the covenant. God would bless Abraham and make him a great nation.

Through Abraham, came the nation of Israel. Israel was a special people unto God. God loved Israel. And in the beginning, Israel loved God. But Israel was a rebellious nation. They were like disobedient children to God — hard-headed and stubborn. They angered God, tempted Him, and persistently rebelled against Him. But even in this, God never forsook His covenant — the covenant He made with Abraham. And as long as Israel remained obedient to God, He blessed them and protected them from their enemies. But God would have to chastise them, and then He would forgive them when they repented and showed Godly sorrow, and He welcomed them back into the fold. God exhibited much grace and mercy with Israel. God truly is a merciful God.

We can learn a lot from David's relationship with God. David loved the Lord with all his heart. This love is expressed in the many songs he wrote. David trusted God, and looked to Him for guidance and direction. And when he sinned against Him by taking Bathsheba and killing her husband, David was genuinely remorseful and repented of his actions. God knew that David's heart was pure. And God loved David because of this. God blessed David, and made him a great king. And God made David's seed to sit upon the throne forever.

Through David's seed would come the Messiah — Jesus Christ — who God would use to bring forgiveness of sins to mankind. Through Jesus Christ the world can be saved. Jesus came to earth preaching a message of repentance from sin. He also introduced the world to the kingdom of God, in all its fullness. Jesus, through His life, showed us how to serve the Father.

## Afterword

Now it's up to you and I. It's now up to the church to be God's earthly representatives on earth. We must allow His word to impregnate us, and His Holy Spirit to indwell us so that the power of the living God will flow out of us, and into the hearts of the unbelieving world so that their unbelieving hearts would be turned to the Lord. More than anything, it is the Lord's desire that all would come to repentance so that none are lost, and that all would be saved.

Jesus will one day make His appearance in the sky; He will call together God's people — His church; a people who have kept themselves unspotted from sin. God has extended His grace and mercy to us. He desires that all are saved. His love for the world was so great that He sent His only begotten Son to save it. And now He has chosen and sent us (the church) into the world to bring the world into the knowledge of the truth.

Our mission is clear. Our purpose has been defined. And all Spirit-filled believers have been empowered by God to fulfill this purpose. But we must allow God complete control of our lives. We must humble ourselves before Him and allow ourselves to be used by Him, for His glory. In the end, God should get the glory out of our lives.

# NAYLA BOOK PUBLISHERS

Thank you for purchasing this book. We pray that you have been blessed by it.

Other Books by Jeanita:

An Open Letter to the Church: On Faith, Holiness, and Being Full of the Holy Ghost

The Purpose of Man: God Created Man and Gave Him Dominion and Authority Over All of His Creation

Step Out of the Shadows: Helping Widows Move Past Grief

Website:
naylabookpublishers.com

Contact:
info@naylabookpublishers.com

www.ingramcontent.com/pod-product-compliance
Lightning Source LLC
Chambersburg PA
CBHW020700300426
44112CB00007B/459